This is my home now
Stories from refugees in Southampton

Based on interviews conducted in 2010/2011

Project Manager MAIANNA MOREAU
Interviews JENNY CUFFE, SHIRLEY FIRTH, XANTHE HACKETT, AURIOL MAYO, MAIANNA MOREAU
Writer JUDITH HENEGHAN
Design ISABEL JAMESON
Published by THIS IS MY HOME NOW
Printed and bound in the UK by M&M Printers

ISBN 978-0-9568963-0-8

Visit us online at WWW.MYHOMENOW.ORG

CONTENTS

FOREWORD

At the moment I am like a blind person, looking for my luck, looking for my life. Can I ever go back to my country? Should I build a life here? Can I ever find someone who loves me but can also understand what happened to me?

Being interviewed for this book has made me think about my life – where I am now and what I need to do next. When other people read my story they might understand a little better too, because until you look inside people's lives, you cannot understand.

Maybe one day my story will become a piece of history and people will see that what happened to me could happen to them, because we are all humans and it does not matter who you are or where you are from, your fate will find you.

Kardo, 25

I felt quite at ease, telling my story. It was moving but not upsetting; tears came but I didn't mind. What happened to me was a long time ago but it is with me all the time, I remember every detail and I am not embarrassed – it is my life.

It helps to tell people all that you have been holding back, to share it with people who believe what you are saying. I feel honoured and privileged that people want to hear my story. If I hadn't come here I would be dead. I am a very lucky person, I have had a lucky life.

Rose, 91

INTRODUCTION

When Rose Dawson, née Lehrman, arrived in Southampton 63 years ago seeking refuge from the Nazis who had invaded her homeland, she was given an identity card with the word 'Alien' stamped on her photograph. When she wanted to travel outside the city centre, she had to get permission from the police. Like all the contributors to *This is my home now*, Rose came to the UK because she had no choice – the alternative was death in a concentration camp – and she left her family and hopes for the future behind. Arriving in Southampton, she set about re-building her life and, at the grand age of 91, she is as much a part of the city as someone born and bred here.

This book is a celebration of the individuals who have fled conflict or persecution and survived, and the corner of Hampshire where they have found sanctuary and which has been enriched by their presence. Those who tell their stories have made long, often dangerous journeys from countries as far apart as Vietnam, Afghanistan, Poland, Uganda and Sierra Leone. The historic and political contexts are different but, whatever the time and place, war and dictatorships look much the same. As a journalist, I have visited countries where power is in the hands of the capricious and cruel, and seen terrifying circumstances that drive people out of their homelands. The vast majority of refugees are herded into large camps in neighbouring states, but a few individuals make their way across continents to Europe and what stands out in the stories recounted here is their determination and courage.

In the past, if refugees came at a time of international crisis like World War II, the expulsion of Asians from Uganda in 1972 or the fall of Saigon three years later, the host community prepared reception committees and temporary shelter. However, some of those who have arrived more recently, perhaps in the back of a lorry after weeks of travelling or by plane on a false visa, have had to wait years to be accepted as legitimate refugees.

In the intervening period – a kind of legal limbo when they are not allowed to work – they have experienced homelessness and

destitution and been forced to rely on the kindness of strangers. It is a tribute to Southampton and its people that, despite the problems and negative publicity attached to being 'asylum seekers', these newcomers show such affection for their adopted city.

Whatever their individual backgrounds and circumstances, the men and women whose stories are told in this book are united by the common experience of upheaval and loss followed by renewal. A recurring theme is that of identity. When everything you know and understand, even your ability to communicate, has been stripped from you, what remains? As you assimilate an alien culture and adopt a new language, do you become a different person?

On gaining Leave to Remain in the UK (that is, officially recognised as refugees under the UN Convention or granted asylum on humanitarian grounds) the participants in this project have set about finding employment and putting down roots. A few of them still fear the vengeful hand of the regimes they have fled and have

asked for their faces and names to be disguised. They have all talked to us eloquently about events that still cause pain and we have consulted them at every stage of the project, relying on their patience and humour.

We use the word 'refugees' reluctantly because they prefer to be identified by their current occupations as teachers, engineers, writers, chefs, community workers, parents or grandparents. Their lives are threaded into the fabric of the city they now call home. As one participant says, 'The past is the past. This is the future.'

Jenny Cuffe

STORIES

I was born in Azerbaijan in 1961. Azerbaijan is a small country, a former republic of the Soviet Union. I am from the mountainous area in the north, on the border between Russia and Georgia. People say it is like Switzerland. When I was a child, everyone worked on collective farms growing tobacco, including my grandmother, whose father had emigrated from Turkey. She was very strong. After she retired, she still did everything from cooking to milking cows.

My father went to Baku, the capital of Azerbaijan, to study to be an accountant; he met my mother there. I loved school and was top of the class. I loved history and literature best though in the end I decided to study chemistry. I did a diploma in chemical engineering and worked for a year in a big silk factory, as well as studying in St Petersburg. I was very happy during that time – I had a job, friends and family. But when the Soviet Union collapsed I lost everything.

As the Soviet Union disintegrated at the end of the 1980s, relations between Azerbaijan and its neighbour Armenia deteriorated, particularly over the region of Nagorno-Karabakh which was within Azerbaijan but whose

population was mainly Armenian. In 1988, almost all Azerbaijani people were forced to leave Armenia.

Up until then there were many Armenians in Azerbaijan and Azerbaijanis in Armenia. We all worked together and were friends. Yet after the problems in Nagorno-Karabakh, everyone became enemies. Lots of people from both sides were taken away or killed.

Then, on 20th January 1990, Soviet special forces attacked the capital, Baku.

If you imagine the end of the world, I think I've seen it already.

If you imagine the end of the world, I think I've seen it already. It was a dark night, very cold. No one was in the street – just a few cars and people shouting 'they are killing us'. People made barricades, defending Baku but the Russians killed over a hundred civilians – ladies, old men, children. There was a curfew but I had to go to work

MINA
REYNOLDS
Azerbaijan - arrived 2003

A young boy, a Russian soldier, pointed a gun at me. He was laughing. I just looked at him and walked on round a corner. Then I fainted into the dirt. Another time I was at the metro station when soldiers started shooting a group of boys. I just lay down, crying with bullets passing over my head. Everyone was full of hate.

A young boy, a Russian soldier, pointed a gun at me.

More violence broke out on 5th May and Mina's mother was assaulted by some refugees from Armenia while trying to help an Armenian neighbour. During the assault she died of a heart attack.

I don't even want to remember that day. I had a miscarriage afterwards, and later my brother was killed in a car crash. It was so horrible. My brother was my best friend, he was everything to me. I still miss him.

Azerbaijan declared independence in 1991 but the country remained in turmoil. For Mina, the turning point came in 1995 after the failure of an armed uprising against the new president.

At that time I was married to a policeman who had fought in the anti-corruption force against the government, but he had disappeared. People started looking for him and came to beat me up. I wanted to escape from Azerbaijan, and because I'd studied in Russia and my mother had Russian relatives I left and went to Rostov. I was very ill though, and the Russians hated people from my country so I couldn't stay there. My best friend looked after me. Then I came to the UK.

For 13 days I was in Croydon, then I was sent to Margate. Now here. I have been in Southampton for six years. I can't remember my first impressions because I was so depressed and confused; my mind was blank. But after a few months I started to realise that I was here, alive, and that I had to do something.

With my feet facing the water I relax and I'm happy.

One of my biggest problems was that I didn't speak English. I'm very sociable but I didn't know anyone and couldn't talk. I had some problems with teenagers – some racist abuse and I was hit in the face – but slowly things got better. Very kind people helped me.

Now I work in a charity shop. I like this work because you can speak to lots of people. Old people are especially talkative and ask lots of questions; it helps me improve my English. I also volunteer as a learning support assistant for CLEAR. But the best thing that has happened to me in Southampton is the International Cookery Exchange. I love all the ladies – they're very friendly; 20 of us from 18 different countries. We all cook traditional meals – Afghan, Portuguese. I have shown them how to cook *plov* – a special Azeri rice dish.

I had some problems but slowly things got better.

I often go for walks in Royal Victoria Park or Weston Shore. When I am depressed or upset it's best to go to the seaside. With my feet facing the water I relax and I'm happy.

I have had a very difficult life but I have always had great help, from God and from people.

OSMAN BAH

Sierra Leone - arrived 2002

Osman Bah was born in a small village in Sierra Leone, west Africa in 1985. At the age of 16 he was helped to escape his country's brutal civil war and came to the UK. He claimed asylum, but his claim was refused and he lived in a state of legal limbo until August 2010 when he was finally granted Indefinite Leave to Remain.

The rebels came at night. Everybody ran.

I've been in Southampton since June 2002. I grew up here. That old life I used to have was very difficult. In the war they took all the strong boys to join the rebellion; the rebels came at night. Everybody ran. I escaped but I lost my family. In England I feel more safe.

I feel proud of myself, you know, talking like this.

When I first arrived I needed an interpreter for everything. I never studied any English – I only read Arabic. But I know that if I study, I'll get qualifications and no one can take that away from me. I started to study English and Computers at Southampton City College. Now I do everything on my own – I never need an interpreter. This is a big change for me. I practise lots at home on my own and I feel proud of myself, you know, talking like this.

For me, the first thing that I did when I lost my own family was to try to make a new family so I married somebody from my country. We lived together and had a daughter. When we split up I was so down I thought about ending my life. But then I said no, I have to try another way.

Now when I see my daughter I try to talk to her in my own language, but at the end of the day she is going to speak good English and have a nice accent. She is born here, and I see how she is growing up. She is really lovely. It's nice seeing her drinking milk any time she wants, learning, playing. I say to her 'you are so lucky' but she is too young to understand all that. When she is grown up she will see. When you are born in Africa you don't have any support, but here she has people looking after her who come and check everything. It's very good.

When they told me I'd got my Leave to Remain I couldn't believe it. I asked myself, is it true that I am free? Is it true that I can go to the job centre and find a job? Is it true that I don't have to be afraid of Immigration? I didn't sleep for three days, but in the end I had the letter in my hand.

They say I am a Southampton boy.

All my friends laugh at me because they say I am a Southampton boy. I am a Southampton football fan. I love Southampton. I spend most of my time in the library or the park and I like the front of the stadium and the seafront. From West Quay you can see a lot of the city, the seafront, the town centre. It's my hometown.

ZOFIA THOROUGHGOOD

Poland - arrived 1948

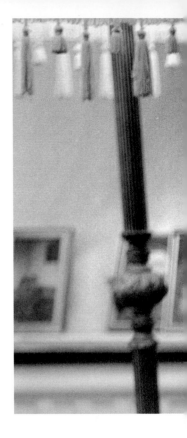

I was born in Maczkowce, in the eastern part of Poland, in 1925 so I am 85 years old. In Maczkowce we had a farm of 16 hectares. We had cows, horses, pigs, chickens, turkeys and geese. My mother used to make quilts; we had to pluck goose feathers for hours. I had one brother and two sisters – there were four of us. When the war broke out I was thirteen. We stopped going to school and I started doing all the work on the farm.

The Russians marched into eastern Poland in 1939. They rounded up hundreds of thousands of Poles and sent them east to labour camps.

I remember the fruit trees beside a big road below our farm. I remember the big tank coming up the hill to find us and I ran like mad, you know, when I saw them. It was really incredible. And of course they started looking for everyone. They pushed my father to the floor with his hands up and told my mother 'You have half an hour to get your children ready.' We didn't know where we were going. It was snowing like hell and it was very, very cold so my mother put warm clothes on and she took the feather quilts and some meat from a pig that was just killed for Christmas and half a loaf of bread.

I remember the big tank coming up the hill to find us.

They put us on trucks and we were going from one neighbour to another; they were collecting everybody and taking them to the train station. They loaded us onto the train and they kept us there for quite a few days. There was no toilet there. We dug a hole in the floor to go to the toilet and of course there were lots of men there... it was dreadful. We waited a long time. And when the train started they told us we were going to Siberia. I'd never heard of it before. Siberia – where was that?

People were dying because they had no food. Our little truck was okay because I think my mother gave some meat to people we knew.

We had the feather quilts which was good, but it is really incredible how we survived. Every so often they opened the doors to throw the dead bodies out.

When the family arrived in Siberia they were given a hut and Zofia had to work cutting down trees in the woods. Her father worked on the river, collecting the logs. They had very little food and while they weren't kept under guard they had nowhere else to go.

The worst part was the illness – typhus.

We were just there and you had to stay there. In fact I met Polish people from the First World War still in Siberia, so we were very lucky to get out. We stayed there for over a year. Then we were put on trains and went to Uzbekistan. In that part of Uzbekistan there was no work, no food – nothing. The worst part was the illness –

typhus. I became very ill and I had the last rites.

In 1941 the USSR joined the Allies in the fight against Germany. Thereafter the USSR came under increasing pressure to deal with its Polish prisoners so, in 1942, tens of thousands of Poles were sent to Iran, now under Allied control, to form Polish combat units.

I can still see Polish soldiers picking us up on stretchers at the hospital and loading us on a train. The whole family was split up. In Tehran my brother went into the army and my sister and I joined the cadets. I wasn't with my parents – they thought I was dead. But I found out that my father was terribly ill in hospital and eventually I was allowed to visit him. He died the next day but at least I saw him. He's buried in Tehran.

Zofia was eventually reunited with her mother and sisters and in 1943 they were shipped out to Tanzania in east Africa. There they lived in a refugee camp with 5,000 other Polish women and children. Zofia went to school and technical college and learned to sew. Then, aged 22, she met a young English sergeant called Ken.

I know I'm British but I still feel Polish.

I wasn't allowed to have any boyfriends at all so we met outside behind the back door and while we were hiding there he stood on an ant nest. He had to take his trousers off because African ants are dreadful and he was screaming with pain because they were biting him and I never laughed so much in my life! That was the first time I met my husband.

We spoke in Swahili because I couldn't speak much English.

We only knew each other for three months, then we got married in Tengeru, in the camp. We spoke in Swahili because I couldn't speak much English. And as soon as we got married we came to Southampton in England – three weeks by boat. We sat on the top deck, the two of us together, so we could kiss.

On arrival in England, Zofia and Ken went to live with Ken's mother in Gillingham before buying a house of their own. Ken joined the Air Force and Zofia soon became pregnant with the first of their two daughters. But language was a problem for Zofia.

I had terrible difficulty. I used to take my address with me when I went for a walk because I thought what if I can't find my way back? But I had to learn to speak. I had to go into shops. There didn't used to be supermarkets, so you had to say what you wanted. Now you just grab things and give them the money – it's so easy!

Eventually she and Ken moved to Southampton to be near the city's large Polish community.

We have been in this house on Stanton Road for 36 years now. We like it very much. Every Wednesday we go to the Polish club. Ken comes with me. We have dinner, we have a Mass, games, exercise. And on Sunday I go to Polish Church. I still buy Polish sausages. I make vegetable soup. I make it on Monday and it lasts the whole week. When my younger daughter and granddaughter and great-grandson come we have soup as well.

I know I'm British but I still feel Polish. I still pray in Polish. We used to go back to Poland every year. Oh, it was incredible to see my family! It was lovely. We used to go every year by car. I haven't been back to the farm though. There's nothing there.

JOANNA HALINA OTTEMBRAJT

Poland - arrived 1946

I was born on 21 September 1940 near Zamasc in eastern Poland. My father was a farmer. In the autumn of 1943 we had to leave the farm and we were transported to Austria.

Going back to Poland was never mentioned. Our land was taken so that was that.

Then when the war ended in 1945 we were pushed onto a goods train and taken to Italy. Going back to Poland was never mentioned. Our land was taken so that was that.

In 1946 we arrived in a refugee camp in Crewe, near Manchester but my father didn't like it very much; it was too industrial. So he moved us down to the Polish refugee camp at Hiltingbury, in Chandlers Ford. We lived at the camp until 1955. It was more rural – lots of open spaces. We used to go for walks in the woods.

Hadi is a poet and writer. He grew up in an educated family in the north of Iran and, at the age of 16, joined a political party which opposed the conservative rule of Ayatollah Khomeini. Many members of his party were executed.

In 1981, aged 16, I was arrested and imprisoned for two years. I wasn't a hero; I wanted excitement. In prison I was with my friends but they killed 16 of them. I was lucky. The judge's wife was my mother's best friend.

I am a writer but this is not a story – it is real.

In 1987 I was arrested again, and again those I was with were all killed. My mother came to visit me in prison. She told me she had been to see a holy woman, and that God would soon send me a message. Well, I laughed. But soon afterwards a bird came into my cell through a tiny hole in the wall. Then, a few days later, I was released. No one

explained why. After 25 years I still don't understand why they didn't kill me.

I still don't understand why they didn't kill me.

In 2005 I was arrested again because by this time I had a website and blog about the Iranian government. I was held in prison for a week and they tortured me very badly – they poured hot water on my leg and hand. I had to go to hospital. However, while I was there I was able to contact my family and they paid money to the hospital guard so that I could get out.

My brothers then found a man in the west of Iran. I went west with that guy and escaped by horse across the mountains to Turkey. When I got to Turkey they put me in a lorry and I travelled to England. When I arrived in London I had no money. My English was so poor.

HADI
KHOJINIAN

Iran - arrived 2005

I found a police station – Paddington station – and applied for asylum. After ten hours they arrested me; they said they had to. But my leg and my hand were very bad so they found a doctor who could speak a bit of Farsi and he sent me to Chelsea Hospital where I stayed for three or four days. After that they sent me to the Home Office in Croydon and then on to Dover – I was there for one month – then to Newport in Wales.

While in Wales I started learning a bit of English and discovered that friends of my brother were living in Southampton. So I moved to Southampton and started working here, in Greek restaurants, in fish and chip shops. Many people helped me. But as an asylum seeker I hadn't got a National Insurance number and then my case failed because they couldn't believe my story. So I started working for charity, helping refugee people, and day after day I began to find myself. I started writing poems and short stories again and, believe me, I've written some lovely poems here. I've got a blog and every day I get around 500-700 visitors from all over the world.

Now, finally, I have an indefinite visa. I hope my family will join me soon – my wife and son. I haven't seen them for five years. I want to start again. I don't want benefits from this country. I love to work and can do anything. I want to open a café bookshop. Imagine – you can come to my coffee shop and start reading a novel and I can give you fresh coffee or Iranian tea. It will be fantastic!

Imagine – you can come to my coffee shop. It will be fantastic!

Seriously I love this country, especially Southampton. Much of it is like my city in the north of Iran. We have docks, a port, sea, forest. Rain, too! Sometimes I feel it's my motherland, this city, because I found myself here. Now I'm just Hadi. I can do anything I want – anything legal. Nobody asks me about my background. English people accept me as I am.

DARUSH

Iran - arrived 2003

Darush was born in Tehran in 1964. When the Shah was deposed and Ayatollah Khomeini came to power in 1979 he was still in high school.

I was so young I didn't support the Shah or Khomeini. I was a teenager, same as my friends, and I thought that maybe Khomeini was a nice man because everyone loved him, but later on I understood my mistake. From the first day he started to kill, kill, kill. His militia started to kill anyone who didn't appear Islamic. I remember two girls, one 16 years old and one 18, on the main road. They had a book and some men stopped in a car and punched them, pushed them inside – bye bye. So I started to read to try to make sense of the revolution. I was asking questions and this led me into trouble. Finally I had to leave the country.

Darush paid a trafficker to take him out of Iran.

I went with my brother to some village near the mountains, and from there I went to some place in Iran by car. But oh my God, to be honest I was so worried they would catch me. It was a very, very, very bad time. Then they put me in a lorry with some others from Turkey and Afghanistan. There was a young family and I could see that a little girl, maybe three years old, was worried – I could see it in her eyes.

He arrived in the UK in 2003.

I saw a police car and waved and asked for help. They took me to the police station for one night and then they took me to some prison – Gosport, I think. The atmosphere there was very, very bad, and I thought oh my God why am I here? But after 24 hours they took me to Immigration in Portsmouth and there someone interviewed me with an interpreter. I told him 'Please, if you want to kill me, kill me here. I don't want to come back to this prison.' And he just laughed. He told me I could stay in a normal place, and I was very, very... I don't know how to explain but I cried a little bit and just said 'Oh my God, thank you, I am free now.'

I cried a little bit and just said 'Oh my God, thank you, I am free now.'

AMINA

Somalia - arrived 2003

I was born in Mogadishu, Somalia in 1968. Mogadishu was a good place then. Our house was right in the centre of town, a big villa built by the Italians. We had all we needed and I had a joyful childhood. My mother raised me with respect and knowledge.

My mother raised me with respect and knowledge.

Then in 1991 President Siad Barre was removed from power and civil war broke out between rival warlords. Over the next 20 years over a million people died as a result of the fighting, famine and disease. Amina fled Mogadishu at the start of the war with her mother and baby daughter.

We knew we had to go out of Mogadishu because it was burning everywhere and one morning there was a very big explosion. One side of our house was burning. I was with my mother and my daughter; my sisters went away with my grandma and uncles. My uncles died

defending them – two of them, the same day. Horrible things were happening. It was a civil war – Darods *[the ruling clan]* against everyone else. I heard later that a lot of my family were killed – my cousins and my brother.

So I left with my baby and my mother and we walked through the night. In day time we had to hide in the middle of nowhere. We stepped on tree roots and things. I was afraid of snakes and that was my nightmare really, thinking I was walking on snakes. We were with a very big group and some men carried water – necessary for children and pregnant women. The journey took 15 days. It wasn't that long. Other people were travelling for months and months and were captured and killed and raped.

We were very lucky although my mother died on the way – she was ill already and she was tired and there wasn't enough food. It was very difficult. My baby sometimes had diarrhoea but I had packets of rehydration powder in my bag so I mixed that with the water I carried and she drank that. We also ate fruit from the trees. I was very strong. I was thinking of my daughter.

I was very strong. I was thinking of my daughter.

When Amina reached Addis Ababa in Ethiopia, she sold her mother's gold and bought a black market visa and a one-way plane ticket to Belgium. From Belgium she travelled by train to Holland and went to a police station there. By now she knew she was six months pregnant but she had lost contact with her husband and the rest of her family.

The people in Holland were very open, very nice. It will stay in my heart forever. I was wearing sandals and my daughter had a little dress with small socks and it was the middle of winter. I can see the lady's eyes – she was a police officer and she was so shocked that she bought a warm suit for the baby right away and she cleaned her and gave me food and I calmed down. She gave me socks and a jacket and drove me to a hotel and I hugged her and said 'thank you very much'. I spoke English and French, thank God. My family were very educated.

After the hotel we went to a small village called Maklo, to a refugee camp with other Somalis. I stayed there for one and a half years. Then I started working there – translating, helping people, learning to speak Dutch. I had my daughter there. Everything was fun and we used to organise fun things like dancing nights.

I was quite young and made some Dutch friends. It was more difficult for the older ones. Later I got a council house and went to university and studied Design. My husband came to Holland too and we had three more children but I couldn't trust him because I found out he had another family so we got divorced.

Then I heard my sister was in Southampton. I also heard that two of my sisters and two brothers were in Ethiopia and one brother was also in England. It was amazing, but at the same time very sad because you think of those who died. Well, anyway, life goes on and you have to move on. So I made the decision to come to the UK in 2003.

We shouldn't let them get away with it. There's no war going on here.

By now Amina had eight children after marrying again. She worked as a cook in a Somali restaurant in St Mary's, moved into a private house and received some income support as well as financial assistance from the other members of her family. She now works for Sure Start in Southampton, is a member of the city council's Muslim Partnership and is chair of the United Somali Community Association as well as a board member of Who Made Your Pants, a local manufacturing project.

The United Somali Community Association helps people really integrate and understand the European way of life – they can combine their own culture with this culture and make it one.

The Muslim Partnership works with the council to advise all the Muslim communities and actually to prevent terrorism and things like that. Somalis run away from their home to feel safe but they are still struggling with their safety. They feel unwanted really and we try to help them understand that the government and most people in society don't hate them.

The rest of society has been a bit too mean towards the Muslim population, especially to women who wear big hijabs. The colour issue's also going on and there are a lot of complaints in the community. A Somali lady went through the park and a young English guy beat her with a cricket bat. It was horrible – her face was swollen so badly. This kind of crime shouldn't happen so I, with the help of the police, explain to people that it's a crime and that they can report it. They can seek witnesses – that's the advice I give them. We shouldn't let them get away with it. There's no war going on here.

ABELARDO CLARIANA-PIGA

Chile - arrived 1977

Abelardo Clariana-Piga was born in Santiago, Chile in 1950. He went to university in Santiago during a period of great political and economic upheaval and took part in a few student demonstrations but did not belong to a political party. Then, in 1975, two years after General Pinochet seized power from President Allende in a military coup, Abelardo was arrested by the secret police.

I don't know exactly why I was arrested. There are two possibilities. When they took me they were carrying this tiny picture of someone. They showed me and asked me if I knew him. I suppose, from the picture, it could have looked a bit like me and I guess they might have arrested me as a result. The other possibility is that I said something against the government to the wrong person and that person told

the military. There were no charges. I went to meet this friend at the place where he worked and they were waiting there – five or six people – secret police. They blindfolded me, put me in the back of the van and drove away, hitting me and threatening me all the while.

I was questioned and tortured a number of times.

I was taken to a secret detention centre. My number was 1024, which gives you an idea of how many people went through there. I was questioned and tortured a number of times – their preferred method was electricity because it did not show afterwards. They asked me stupid questions about who in my family voted for the Communist Party or Allende. I just kept saying 'I don't know. I don't know anything' and obviously they didn't believe it. It was a difficult time.

After two weeks I was transferred to a place called Tres Alamos where they had lots of political prisoners but where you could receive visits from family and your name appeared officially as detained. The Red Cross had access to this camp and you could read the newspaper and listen to the radio. All the prisoners talked politics there every day! In many ways it was easier to be inside because the military had responsibility for us and they couldn't just kill us. We were more worried about what would happen when we were released because some people were being released and then disappearing or being killed by the secret police. On one occasion we went on hunger strike to show that we knew what was going on.

I am a foreigner here and if I returned to Chile I would be a foreigner.

The Pinochet regime came under increasing international pressure over its political prisoners, and in 1976 Abelardo and most of his fellow inmates were freed.

We were certainly very happy when we were freed, but it was very difficult. Now we had to be careful about what we said, and lots of people didn't want to say hello because they feared getting into trouble themselves. Also, the secret police were the ones who decided who could study or get a job. Rumours came round thick and fast about who had been taken, or disappeared. I just wasn't brave enough to stay and I didn't want to put others at risk. So I came to England in 1977. I was given refugee status.

Although I came to study at university here I was not a student – I was a refugee. I had to go through police registration and they gave me this green card and I had to tell them every time I moved. Then, after some years I was given permanent residence. I could have gone back to Chile at any point but I got married and we adopted a child from Chile. Now I have a life here, a commitment. When I finished my degree I applied for a job at Brockenhurst College and I'm still there, full time, though our home is in Southampton.

Our daughter Marcella is 25 now. She sees herself as English, but I am a foreigner here and if I returned to Chile I would be a foreigner. I do miss the country – these long, cold dark winters... oh I don't like it! But you get used to it and you grow old. I had lived in Chile as a youngster. I was a different person. The country has changed, I have changed. I don't feel this urge to go back.

SIXPENCE
MUTAMBO
Zimbabwe - arrived 2006

To claim asylum is not an easy thing. It is the same as going into a cell and locking yourself in there. People find so many reasons why they don't want me here. It's as if they think I'm going to steal all the riches of this country, or maybe prevent half a million people from getting food. But asylum seekers are not allowed to go to work and cannot go to school. It is a technical way of torturing you. You are just waiting; you don't know what is going to happen to you.

To claim asylum is not an easy thing.

As an asylum seeker, Sixpence was not permitted to work but he volunteered for three local charities including the League of Friends at Southampton General Hospital. His duties included selling newspapers and snacks to patients.

If someone knows you are an asylum seeker, he takes you to be a useless person who doesn't even think. But when you are at the hospital doing voluntary work, he doesn't know about your life. If you smile, he starts smiling. He isn't going to ask 'What do you do for a living?' He is the person who asks 'Do you have a Daily Echo?' It makes me forget all those things that worry me.

I couldn't bring
my daughter with
me. I didn't have
a passport for her
and I didn't have
any means for
bringing her over.

SIPHIWE

Zimbabwe - arrived 2003

I was born in 1965 in Matabeleland, in a place called Lupane. In September 1999 I came to the UK to visit my sister for a couple of months. While I was here I became unwell and was hospitalised and I couldn't travel for quite a long time. When I was better I went back to Zimbabwe.

However, Zimbabwe's President Robert Mugabe and his Zanu-PF party were determined to crush any opposition to their one-party regime. From 1999 onwards their methods were increasingly ruthless.

At that time things were getting bad; it wasn't the Zimbabwe we grew up in. Things were really changing and it wasn't nice. People thought maybe I was a spy for the opposition party. I told them I wasn't; I'm not politically involved at all but speaking to Zanu-PF is like speaking to a brick wall. Once they have their minds set on something, that's it, no matter what you tell them.

In January 2003 I was physically assaulted. They told me that if I didn't have a Zanu-PF card next time they came, I'd be in deep trouble. That's when I fled and came here.

I couldn't bring my daughter with me. I didn't have a passport for her and I didn't have any means for bringing her over. I wish I could be with her. It's very hard.

It has taken seven years for my claim to be accepted.

ANITA & BONGEKA

Zimbabwe - arrived 2000 & 2002 respectively

Anita and her daughter Bongeka come from Matabeleland. Anita came to Southampton on a church scholarship in 2000, hoping to gain experience that would enable her to start an orphanage and help disabled children. But on a return visit to Zimbabwe she was attacked by members of the ruling Zanu-PF party and this forced her to seek asylum in the UK. She now works with young people suffering from autism and is doing an Open University course in health and social care.

As soon as Zimbabwe is okay, I will go back.

My hope is to go back to Zimbabwe one day. I even keep saying that to Bongeka, that she should sort herself out, get settled, because as soon as Zimbabwe is okay, I will go back. Not that I don't have a life here, I certainly do. I've got a lot of friends; I've got so much more going for me really. But I just keep thinking of going back, before I get too old. I think it's about roots. My mind is just there, really. And maybe it's the fact that I've always wanted to do something.

I am trying to save a little bit for my orphanage project. I've got stuff like curtains and linen and I've even got toys – boxes and boxes of toys. Obviously I'd feel a bit lonely because people there have moved on and grown apart. It will be another new start but at least then I'd achieve my goal. Because I think people in Zimbabwe need more help than here, you know. I'll be more useful there.

Bongeka joined her mother in the UK when she was 12 years old. She is studying at Southampton City College and hopes to run her own nursery one day and travel the world.

I'd rather go forward.

If my mum went back to Zimbabwe I'd stay here. This is my home. Yes I would love to go and visit there, but I can't stop my life again and re-start it again. I'd rather go somewhere new – maybe the States, or Canada, or anywhere. I'd rather go forward.

The Polish Social Club,
Portswood, Southampton

HABIB
AHMADI

Afghanistan - arrived 2001

Habib grew up in a remote mountain village in central Afghanistan. He belongs to the Hazara ethnic group of Shia Muslims who were persecuted by extremist Taliban forces in the 1990s.

I am from Oruzgan, in central Afghanistan. It's a very lovely, beautiful place, though the winters are very hard – you could walk straight from the roof of our house to the top of the snow. I was born on 13 March 1984. My family are Hazara.

I'm proud to be Hazara. I think Hazaras are hard working people. We used to buy very little from the town. Most things we produced ourselves on our small farms: oil, meat, wheat – quite a lot of stuff. But before I left it was a bad time. Something hard happened there. I was left alone and I had to move – there was no choice.

What is happening in Afghanistan is all politics. It's a game – a dirty game. Everywhere in Afghanistan in the name of the Mujahideen and in the name of Jihad, people committed genocide against innocent people. These people are still alive, still walking around. They still put their heads up and call themselves the future of Afghanistan. They have the power there.

I tell you, when I got to the tunnel I cried.

So in '95 or maybe '97 I made the journey to Pakistan, then Iran, then Turkey. We paid mafia people and they showed us the way. It was a big move, a big shock. I remember the mountains on the border with Turkey. There were about 100 of us and we were very hungry. Four died in front of my eyes because of the food, because of the water, because of the hardness of the journey. In Turkey we hid in an ice-cream freezer to get past one of the police stations. It was nearly four months to Istanbul and when we got there I was passing blood; I was so dehydrated.

After some days in Istanbul they moved us to a place where we could get on a container ship. About 350 of us got inside. There was no water. We went to Italy, then to France. In France I spent several days on trains but I walked the last part to Sangatte camp. I was so scared... I tell you, when I got to the tunnel I cried.

It was so mad. I would definitely not try again – you're playing with your life. It's like a suicide – definitely the same, the way people are moving, coming, claiming asylum. It's like you are actually touching the button – every minute you could blow yourself up. You don't know the people around you.

Habib applied for asylum when he arrived in Kent and was eventually granted Indefinite Leave to Remain. He worked as a waiter before moving to Hook and working in a factory making cardboard boxes for bouquets. He was soon promoted, and then moved to jobs as a logistics supervisor at a salad packing plant in Bognor Regis and a team manager for a company in Andover while studying for a diploma in management.

It is critical to know the language. If you don't know how to speak, you can't defend yourself. But I like England; I like the way people are organised. I had the opportunity to study here, get married. I have a family now. It was hard to move, a big challenge, but I am Habib. I know myself now. I can manage myself, my family. I can help others around me.

I am Habib. I know myself now.

Quite a lot of people know me here. I live in Southampton, I get involved in the community; I am very proud. But I do think I want to go back to Afghanistan. A lot of people in Afghanistan are lost, depressed and upset. I want people to know what's happening around them. This is our future. I want people to get involved in that process; to participate properly in elections, go to school, be strong. Let's work together. We can do it.

AFIFA

Afghanistan - arrived 2003

Afifa's family fled from Afghanistan when the Russians invaded in 1979. Afifa was educated in Pakistan and worked for several international humanitarian organisations including Save the Children UK, which invited her to London to receive an award from Princess Anne. But her views on women's rights put her in danger in Pakistan and, in 2003, she returned to the UK to seek asylum.

I said 'I can tell you they are Afghans and you should not shout at them.'

At Heathrow I gave in my passport and applied for asylum. I was treated very well there because they checked my records and said 'Oh, you came to the UK last year and you were invited by Princess Anne. What made you come back?' And I was treated nicely compared to the other asylum seekers.

There were maybe five or six at that time. Immigration officers were shouting at them, saying 'We know you are not Afghans, you are Pakistanis and you are saying you are Afghans and claiming asylum.' So I went to them and I said 'I can tell you they are Afghans and you should not shout at them.' They were a bit surprised.

That night I had to sleep in the airport under a bench without a blanket. Then I was sent to a hotel where there were about 500 asylum seekers and then I had an interview at the Home Office. A week later I was sent to Southampton where I got my visa and applied for my National Insurance number.

Depression and anxiety are very common among refugees and asylum seekers. I started working for Solent Mind, running sessions about mental health for refugees and asylum seekers at City College and other venues. Now I work for Solent NHS Trust.

I have independence which I would not have in Pakistan and Afghanistan as a woman.

I have independence which I would not have in Pakistan and Afghanistan as a woman. I am proud to be a British citizen.

Edgar Feuchtwanger is a historian who spent most of his academic career at the University of Southampton. He was born to a Jewish family in Munich in 1924 and for a time lived in the same street as Hitler.

He [Hitler] just moved into this block of flats which was about 100-150 yards away from us on the opposite side of the road. I did once remember seeing him walking there... I was taken for a walk, I was still perhaps eight or nine years old and he came out of his house to get into his car; he was wearing a mackintosh with a belt, and he had something like a Trilby hat on. There were a few people around and they shouted 'Heil Hitler' and possibly even gave a salute, and he just lifted his hat a little bit like anybody might and got into the car.

Of course, by '35, '36 he travelled with a large entourage of SS bodyguards who had taken over the flat at the bottom of the block. The chauffeurs would sit in the cars, these long Mercedes cars which you see in the newsreels, and then suddenly the engines would start up and the SS bodyguards would come out of the house and take their seats in the cars. You heard their boots on the pavements as they

rushed out and then, quickly after that, he came out, gave a cursory salute and got in beside the driver, which nobody important does now, and the cavalcade rushed off.

Suddenly the engines would start up and the SS bodyguards would come out.

The Feuchtwanger family knew that the Nazis were deeply anti-Semitic, but they had another reason to fear their rise to power. Edgar's uncle Lion Feuchtwanger had written a satirical novel, Erfolg, *about the rise of the Nazis.*

Erfolg is a panoramic novel set in Bavaria in the early 1920s. It portrays Hitler as a garage mechanic with the gift of the gab. It's a very hard-hitting satirical book, so nowadays it's a cult novel in Germany. It was the first novel by a well-known writer about the rise of the Nazis. My uncle always read his books out to people,

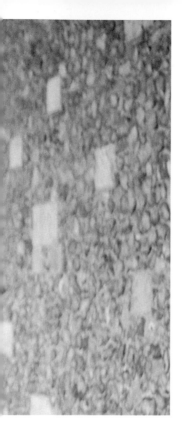

EDGAR FEUCHTWANGER

and he read out bits to my father and my father thought 'Oh my God!' and then when it came out of course it created a great stink and Goebbels wrote in his journal: 'We'll see to you when we get to power.' So the amazing thing is that my parents and my uncle thought they could live a moment longer in Nazi Germany. Nowadays, you'd take the first flight out. But people thought, Germany is a civilised country, it's got the rule of law. They couldn't quite grasp what a switch it was.

The turning point came, as it did for many German Jews, on 9th November 1938, known as Kristallnacht or the Night of Broken Glass. Jewish properties and homes were destroyed and 30,000 Jewish men were rounded up and sent to concentration camps.

[was 14. What I remember of it most is that, in the morning, my father was taken away to the concentration camp, Dachau, and then a whole posse of people and removal vans arrived and they took away his library. At that point the whole action was intended to frighten Jews and get them to see that they must get out of Germany. And

so actually he was released in time for Christmas. But of course it was painfully obvious then that we couldn't possibly stay there.

It was painfully obvious that we couldn't possibly stay there.

Edgar and his family were eventually able to obtain visas to come to the UK because they had relatives abroad who could pay the £1,000 required by the Home Office. Edgar was sent out ahead of his parents and spent some time with family friends in Cornwall before they heard that Winchester College was prepared to take three refugee boys.

It was September 1939. My parents had come over in May but I did not live with them. They probably thought it was better if I lived in an English atmosphere, not with them, and so it was. My father was interned for three months on the Isle of Man. My mother of course moved heaven and earth to get him out which she managed to do. He wasn't there all that long.

45

It's fear of the outsider, and I suppose that's what the Jews suffered from.

At Winchester I was in Chernocke House on the corner of Southgate Street and Romans Road. In the basement we had bunks which we had to go to now and then when there were raids on Southampton and Portsmouth. The Holocaust wasn't clear to people then; the war and the fighting were in the forefront but I think people knew that Jews were persecuted. Some of the more intellectual boys got a newspaper out and I wrote a piece called *Munich Diary* in which I described how I saw Hitler and other things.

After Winchester, Edgar was conscripted to do forestry work and was sent to Savernake Forest in Wiltshire where he worked in a saw mill. After this he took up a scholarship to Magdalen College, Cambridge and was naturalised as a British citizen in 1947.

For me it would have been almost impossible to go back to Germany. Germany wasn't a healthy sort of place in 1946-7. My father seriously considered going back but my mother wasn't keen on it. Anyway my father died. That was 1947.

Edgar began teaching at the University of Southampton, where he remained until he retired in 1989. He married, had a family, wrote a number of history books and set up a long-standing link between the University of Southampton and the University of Frankfurt. From his home in the village of Dean he reflects on the plight of more recent refugees.

You know so many people are basically hostile, aren't they? To anyone who comes in – economic migrant or asylum seeker. They may be slightly less hostile to asylum seekers but they're sceptical and think it may be a sham and so on. That sort of thing makes me feel uneasy, you know. It's fear of the outsider, and I suppose that's what the Jews suffered from though I think one's got to be a bit careful because the German Jewish situation was so specific. It was so tied up with ideology.

Since declaring independence from France in 1958, Guinea has been ruled by a series of autocratic presidents and endured systemic corruption and violence.

My father had a tyre business in Conakry. He imported tyres from Europe and the business was successful – too successful. The government knew it and blocked everything so he lost all his money. He tried to fight his case but in the end he ran away because if you fight the government, they might kill you.

Djoulde's father fled Guinea and came to the UK in 2004. He was granted Indefinite Leave to Remain and 16-year old Djoulde and the rest of his family followed in 2007. Djoulde now studies electrical engineering at Eastleigh College.

I don't go out much, but I have a job at British Home Stores and I have paid for driving lessons. The police have stopped me ten times, asking me if I was drunk, but I don't drink! It's a good control though, because a lot of people drive and drink and then crash, or drive without insurance. They have these controls for your safety. In Guinea you can drive when you are five if your parents have money and they let you. It is unbelievable.

If you fight
the government,
they might kill you.

DJOULDE

Guinea - arrived 2007

The Bargate,
Southampton city centre

VÂN
THI-NGUYEN

Vietnam - arrived 1984

I was born in Vietnam in 1952, outside Saigon, now Ho Chi Minh City. My mother was a half-Cambodian village girl and my father was a captain in the French Army, which at that time was in control of Vietnam. They weren't married – it's a painful story for my mum. My father just took her and when she was pregnant with me, he went back to France.

The French were forced to withdraw from Vietnam in 1954 and the country split into the communist-controlled north and a regime of former French supporters, backed by the US, in the south. But the communists, or Vietcong, began to assert control in the south using a range of guerrilla tactics.

I grew up in a small village in the south of the country. The communists came to live in our village and watched us. They were fighting the government. They would take our food or make the young ones work on the road – dig a hole and put explosives in. We were very frightened but there was nothing you could do.

My mum and step dad had a farm – a good farm. But when I was ten years old the communists came and took them to the forest, beat them and demanded money. They tried to strangle my mum. So the next morning my step dad, who was too hurt to work, had to sell everything to get money before they came back. Then we ran for our lives. If we stayed we would have been killed. We left that home and went up to Saigon.

If we stayed there we would have been killed.

In Saigon my step dad had no job. I had to leave school and go out and find work. I was eleven years old. At first I helped a lady sell fish in the market. There were American soldiers in Saigon at that time and I had a picture of my dad. He looked like them. I dreamed that they'd say 'I'm your father' but it didn't happen. It was just a dream.

In her late teens Vân met a man who became her husband but the marriage didn't last and Vân was left with a young baby – her son, Hieu. Then she met someone else and became pregnant again, but as the Vietcong

took control, the situation worsened. A series of offensives from the north finally led to the withdrawal of US troops and the fall of Saigon in 1975. Millions of South Vietnamese began to flee the country.

I worked in the black market buying and selling jewellery. I was quite successful at that but I couldn't do what I wanted to do, I couldn't get a job because the communists from the north treated us like dogs. I was the enemy because my father was French and although my new man was Vietnamese he had worked for the old government. We were frightened that we would end up in prison. So when I got the chance to get out and go to France, I went.

I was the enemy because my father was French.

It was August 1977. Hieu was five years old already, and I was eight months pregnant. I got a letter from the French Embassy to say I had a visa. Hieu too. But when they saw I was pregnant they said I couldn't go so I said I was only six and a half months – I was very slim – and a French doctor examined me and signed the paper.

Vân had to leave without her new baby's father. He had a wife and family already but eventually left Vietnam and made his way to the UK. Vân, meanwhile, arrived in Paris and had her baby, a boy called Michel. She settled there for a few years, learned French and worked as a cleaner in a factory but eventually she brought Michel and Hieu over to the UK, to Sholing, to be with Michel's father and his five other children. It wasn't easy, with seven children to care for.

I worked for a long time with a lot of cleaning jobs while I trained as a chef at Bournemouth College and then spent two years at technical college in St Mary's. After that I opened a takeaway shop. I am a survivor. Wherever you put me, I will learn and go out to work and look after myself. My husband died eleven years ago and now I just work in the daytime, at St Anne's school as an assistant in the Food Technology classroom. I am also learning to dance with a group of English friends – ballroom, Latin, jive. My children are all quite near.

The past is the past; this is the future.

England is my home now. If I go on holiday I feel homesick – I just have to go back to England with all the green parks! It's a wonderful feeling you know. In my mind I still wonder if I will be moved on again to another country. I hope not. The past is the past; this is the future. I am healthy and I'm lucky.

In DR Congo they try to kill history. They don't want the past to stay.

CHARLES & ELODIE

Democratic Republic of Congo - arrived 2003 & 2005 respectively

DR Congo (formerly Zaire) is one of Africa's largest countries with vast mineral resources but in the last 15 years several million people have died as a result of the conflict between the government and rebels backed by neighbouring states. In 2002 Charles was working as a telephone engineer in the capital, Kinshasa when the government made false accusations against him.

My job was to fix telephones for officials from the government, police, military staff and so on. But life began to change after the death of President Laurent Kabila *[in 2001]*. The people accused of killing Kabila were put on trial, and because I had installed a telephone for them they said I had tried to help them.

Elodie recalls the day they came to arrest Charles.

When they came to arrest my husband he was not at home. I tried to phone him. I said 'don't come home again' because I was afraid they would kill him. I had six children and I was pregnant but I was afraid and stressed and had a miscarriage.

To escape arrest, Charles was forced to leave his wife and children and flee. After gaining asylum in the UK he was reunited with his family in 2005.

When I saw my children it was a very joyful day.

Charles, Elodie and their children all now have British citizenship. However, it hasn't been easy settling in to a new life, a new climate and a new culture, as Charles observes.

I miss the friendship. Here you can spend two days without visiting a friend. In my country I don't have to call first to say I'm coming. We just go and visit and we are welcome. Here we have to find out if our friend is at home, and ask if it is okay to visit and often friends say 'oh no, sorry, we are going out' so it's a big problem.

We have to accept it's a new life, a new culture.

Here, sometimes, even in the church you cannot say hello to someone. In my country when you know this guy, this lady, we pray together so for me it's like sister and brother. It's a strong relationship. But here, no. So all this is very, very different and we have to accept it's a new life, it's a new culture. There is an English couple living in Hythe – they are our best friends. I know we cannot meet every day but they have tried to help us understand English culture. I will feel really British when I've got a job. Then I can pay tax and I can really say I'm British.

Yet Charles also sees a positive side to life in the UK.

I think safety is better here. When I see people on TV sometimes saying bad things to David Cameron and they are free, I always say 'You are blessed.' Because in my country if you say 'Kabila is not good, Jean Bemba is not good' you are arrested and killed. Every time I try to explain Southampton to my friends I say 'You know about the Titanic? I'm living in the same town where the Titanic came from.' In DR Congo they try to kill history. They don't want the past to stay.

CHARLENE

Democratic Republic of Congo - arrived 2005

Charles and Elodie's eldest daughter Charlene is now studying law at Southampton Solent University.

Coming here is a very positive thing. I miss my cousins and my grandparents but I have my mum, my dad, my brothers and sisters and I have found a lot of my old friends from Congo using Facebook. I am English now! My father likes us to speak French at home, but my younger brothers and sisters prefer to speak English. When they start arguing it's in English.

I have found a lot of my old friends from Congo using Facebook.

I want to be a lawyer. I am tempted to go into immigration law, and I've been doing work experience with the CLEAR project in Southampton. I think I would be good because I speak three languages – I might end up helping someone who speaks French or Lingala.

GRACE

Democratic Republic of Congo - arrived 2003

Grace was born and raised in Kinshasa and worked in a restaurant there. When a customer offered her one hundred dollars to distribute some political leaflets, she agreed. She had no idea of the impact this would have on the rest of her life.

I was taken by men in uniform, put in a house and abused in every way possible. I was so badly beaten – all the rape and all that. I didn't know what was happening. But when a new guard came he saw me bleeding and took me to hospital. Then my boyfriend talked to one of the doctors and he made it possible for me to leave the hospital and flee the country. I travelled with the agent – the one we paid to get me out. We didn't have enough money for my boyfriend to come with me. He was killed later.

We didn't have enough money for my boyfriend to come with me. He was killed later.

Grace arrived in Dover in 2003 and claimed asylum. After being placed in detention and questioned for three days she was eventually sent to Southampton where she was given some subsistence support, but after six months her claim was refused and this was withdrawn. She did, however, receive counselling from Rape Crisis and became the first client to receive financial support from SWVG during the long period of uncertainty about her status.

It was difficult, because you don't know; maybe, maybe not, maybe, maybe not. But I had hope. I just knew that one day it would be fine because here I never felt as scared as I did in my own country. Here they talk but no one will beat me. No one will do all the bad stuff they can do to you in my country. Even when they refused me asylum *[Grace's claim was turned down several times]* I knew it would be better because the future had to be brighter than the way it was before.

Then, in 2010, Grace was finally granted Leave to Remain.

I think you will always have some people who are very kind, and you always find people who are really against why you've come here. I didn't have a lot of that, but you will have them in the process you have to go through. Mostly though, people were fine – they were kind to me.

Haider was born in Baghdad in 1967, one of three children. His parents were academics, working in the physics departments of the city's two universities.

Childhood was great back in the 70s when I was about five. We had a lovely villa in a leafy area of Baghdad with a river close by. It was a wonderful neighbourhood. Palm trees, all my friends in the neighbourhood on bicycles, sleeping on the roof. We played hop scotch with the girls, cops and robbers, skate boards, roller skates, football. I had a silver chopper from Scotland because in 1975 the whole family went to Dundee while Mum studied for her Masters degree there.

We had a lovely villa in a leafy area of Baghdad.

My dad was a clever man and in 1978 he was invited to open the physics department in the Emirates at the newly established university. So Mum and Dad decided to re-locate. Emirates was

exciting – a lovely Islamic country, full of different nationalities.

While the family was living in Emirates, Saddam Hussein became leader of the Ba'ath Party and President of Iraq and the Iran-Iraq war broke out. Haider's mother's Iranian ancestry made it dangerous for the family to return to Baghdad.

All of my grandparents were born in Baghdad, but their families were from Persia so our origins were in Iran, which Iraq was fighting unfortunately. I know many stories: cousins of my mother were big merchants and were basically put on the border barefoot with their watches and jewellery pulled off their wrists, pushed away and told to go home. This happened to hundreds of thousands of people, not just the Persians. I mean, there were a lot of Iraqis who were killed or went missing, just because they didn't understand or accept the way the government was ruling the land.

A lot of people knew what was going on. It was quite clear that Iraq wasn't safe as soon as Saddam started executing people, deporting people, making war with Iran. My mum's passport showed her Persian connections. She couldn't go back. It was very, very sad.

HAIDER
AL-HUSSAINI

Iraq - arrived 1983

It was quite clear that Iraq wasn't safe.

Eventually Haider's parents decided to move to England. His father took a job at the University of Southampton and they bought a house in Upper Shirley. Haider was 16 when they arrived and after O levels and A levels he went to catering college at St Mary's. But he wanted to travel, and needed a passport.

We weren't welcome at the Iraqi embassy. It wasn't easy because of the political situation and the whole system was a shambles. It wasn't just my family – I think millions of people were sort of in this limbo. Iraqis in Canada, in Sweden, in the US. They were all stuck, really.

We could have applied for asylum, but my father didn't think this was necessary for a man in his position. I think we were advised that if we stayed out of trouble and if we had enough time and enough finances behind us, then we could become nationals.

I think it took about ten years – ten long years – but when the time came we just had to submit the request, sort out finances and have an individual interview. It was very informal, pleasant, done in our home. We had an appointment with the lawyer for 20 minutes. I swore on the Qu'ran, just to show I was telling the truth.

You get citizenship first, and then you apply for a passport. Three days after getting my passport I was on a Greek island, enjoying the heat that I never had in ten years in Southampton. It reminded me of Baghdad actually. I haven't stopped travelling since.

After a few years of working in the catering industry and travelling in his holidays, Haider opened Fountains Cafe in Southampton's Civic Centre.

The business was already there, but it had been closed for two years. So I submitted a business plan with Mohammed my brother. I just had to invest a few thousand and then I competed with some other companies for the lease, which I won. It's a great, great feeling. I'd recommend it to anybody who wants to work for themselves.

I'm honoured when someone from another culture comes and teaches me something.

You don't have to be too greedy to be happy in terms of money or success – you just need a little bit of control. I'm very happy here. I have my friends, my business. I'm meeting new people and there's a really healthy mix of cultures.

When I see the refugees, I feel for them but sympathy is not enough. I'd like to talk to them, I'd like to help them; I have helped in the past. I'm honoured when someone from another culture comes and teaches me something. For some reason, Iraqis see me as a figure in the city. Maybe I'm developing into one. It comes with age and hopefully people respect me enough to come in and ask me for advice and assistance.

Many different people seek me out – Romanians, Polish. If they need a bed for the night or a mattress somewhere, I'll help. If they need a meal, I'll help but I'm not interested in breaking the law. I think these things could somehow be monitored a little better, people given more opportunities, in a sensible way. I'd love to be President for a week or a year. Why not? I'd tidy things up.

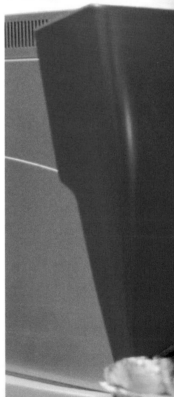

KARDO

Iraq - arrived 2004

Kardo was born in 1987 in the Kurdish region of northern Iraq but grew up in Baghdad. When US-led coalition forces invaded Iraq in 2003, the regime of Saddam Hussein was toppled and in the violence and unrest that followed his father disappeared and his mother was shot dead in the street. Kardo was 18 years old.

After my mother was killed my uncle said I had to move – I couldn't stay in his house because it was too dangerous. He took me to a friend's house in a village. Then he said I'd have to leave the country.

'We don't know each other. You didn't pay me and you know nothing.'

I don't know how my uncle found a smuggler to take me to Europe. He paid cash – over a thousand dollars. We kissed each other and he said goodbye. Then someone came with a van that went round picking people up – none of us knew each other. We were told to be silent – more than ten of us in a small van. We crossed the border into another country. The guy who took us said 'We don't know each other. I'm not your boss. You didn't pay me and you know nothing.'

The driver went very fast. We drove for over 24 hours through the hills and villages – someone was crying that it wasn't safe. Then we got to a safe place with showers and nice food, and we stayed for a few days. We mixed with another group travelling from Iraq. They spoke a different language. The driver said he'd get a big lorry for all of us. We left at night – 40 or 50 people in the lorry – some being sick, some crying, some screaming, some fainting. I was in the corner. We heard shooting and the driver told us to calm down and stay quiet. He kept going. We arrived in a forest and we had to get out one by one and walk.

I walked for a long time – many hours. It was night; I saw nothing. Then I got to a small house and slept there. All the others were older. I was the only young person. Then I got a phone call from my uncle.

I couldn't believe it. I told him I loved him and asked about my sister. He said she was okay and that I would be taken to a safe place in Europe.

I was driven in a small car, then another lorry. I had no idea where I was going. The lorry felt like it was on a ship. Someone else made a hole and we looked out and saw lorries all around us. The ship made a booming noise, like the Titanic. I wondered if we would die.

When we came out of the lorry I got in another car. The driver told me not to ask any questions. Some people said we were in Italy. Others said France, but it was Greece. We stayed there for one month. An older guy took care of me; my uncle had asked him to keep me safe. Then one night the guy put me on a lorry to Holland with three others. We hid in a space inside the lorry for four days and nights. No toilet. I couldn't eat much.

When we arrived in Holland we stayed in a house overnight and then got into one last lorry. I didn't know where I was going. The lorry drove onto another ship. It was cold. People were sick and one man was crying like a baby. I cried as well.

After a few more days I was dropped off at a petrol station near Southampton. The driver told me to ask for the police, but it was night time. I didn't know anybody. I saw the cars going *vroom, vroom* past me.

I was dropped off at a petrol station near Southampton.

I went into the petrol station. I couldn't speak English – just a few words. My face was dirty, black. I hadn't eaten. I was tired and I just fell down. I said 'Police!' and the guy there helped me. He gave me water and biscuits. Then the police came.

Kardo spent four days at the police station. A social worker was assigned to him and he was placed in temporary accommodation but after two months he was told

After three years I have to send my documents back to the Home Office but I hope I get permission to stay here forever and have a happy life.

he would be sent back to Holland because this was the country he had left to come to the UK. Afraid and isolated, he ran away.

It's not easy here – I didn't know the law. I didn't know anybody. I didn't speak English. So I left the house, I left the social worker, I left everything. I slept in a park, then my friend let me stay with him. I washed cars sometimes for ten pounds a day so that I could get shopping for us both. For three years I had this terrible life and I was very depressed. It was a hard situation; I had seen my mother die. I was fighting with my brain.

Kardo eventually made contact with several local charities including Pathway and SWVG, and they petitioned the local MP. He has since been given Leave to Remain for three years in the UK.

Now I live in Portswood in Southampton and my job is in Southampton as well. I'm working in a restaurant as a chef and I'm in charge and I pay insurance, I pay tax, everything. I'd love to have my own business. I like hairdressing, but also I'd just love to have my own restaurant and be a chef and have a beautiful wife and two or three nice kids.

Sometimes I think about the past. What has happened to me is unbelievable. The only thing I have to say is thanks to God so much and all the people who helped me. After three years I have to send my documents back to the Home Office but I hope I get permission to stay here forever and have a happy life. That's what I wish.

KUSUM & JAYESH
ASHER

India/Uganda - arrived 1972

Kusum Asher was born in Gujarat, India in 1938, the youngest of five sisters and two brothers. She took her O levels and started work as a teacher before marrying a Hindu man and settling in Uganda. For ten years she lived happily in the capital, Kampala, with her husband and three young children. Then one morning in August 1972, everything changed.

We woke up and General Amin announced that all 'non-citizens' had to leave the country. All British people had to leave. Well my husband had a Ugandan passport so we thought OK we are all right, even though I had a British passport. But when my husband went to Immigration to check they took his passport and told him he was stateless; he was not allowed to leave.

Kusum was eventually allowed to leave for the UK with her children. Her husband was able to follow her with a new British passport two weeks later, though almost all of their money was taken from them. Jayesh, Kusum's second child, was seven at the time.

I remember the refugee camps we stayed in when we first arrived in the UK. It was quite an exciting time for a child. We were free and I remember a very nice chef – he used to give the kids treats and I think that went a long way in making us feel at home in such an alien environment. It was the first time we'd had fried egg! And it was cold, very cold, and people from Oxfam came with handouts of clothes, gloves and hats – I'd never seen gloves before. The barracks was a big building and we could explore it with the other children. Each family got its own room and own bed and everything. I also remember my father arriving. I think much credit must be given to my mother because as a child I never felt afraid.

It was cold, very cold. I'd never seen gloves before.

After one week in the UK, Kusum started work in a thermos factory in Newhaven. They remained in the barracks for six weeks until they found a council house in Totton. Then Kusum's husband also found work. Jayesh remembers the welcome they received.

I remember when we first got there some people had left a box of toys which was really nice. I remember getting the toys out and

My children are born in this country, they're British, yet I bring them up in our culture. There's always that fine balance to achieve.

playing with them, for many years. I've got good memories of that house, of growing up there. I think that's why we kept it. There were lots of children around, a big green at the back of the house, and we'd meet other kids after school and kick a football around.

The primary school we went to was Oakfield. They put us in different classrooms and they gave us a buddy so we could make friends quickly. From there we went to Testwood, where I became head boy. Then I went to Totton College. I went on to University in Bradford and became a pharmacist and came back here to work in Totton, so I've gone the full circle.

Nowadays I see a lot of people I grew up with, and they still come into the shop or ask me how my mother is. My brother lives in America now and he's quite nicely settled, but whenever I talk to him he still asks me what the football scores are, how Southampton is doing. So in his heart, he still belongs here.

Nevertheless, growing up it was hard to pinpoint where you belonged. There was one life when you were at school with your friends and another life when you came home. There was that sort of duality going on – still is. My children are born in this country, they're British, yet I bring them up in our culture. There's always that fine balance to achieve.

Kusum acknowledges this balance.

My husband passed away in 1994, but I'm still working. I do one day in Oxfam and two days in the British Heart Foundation in Winchester, and on Wednesday I help at the Asian Welfare Centre in Eastleigh. This is my country. I always call myself British. I am Indian, but I am British Indian.

SHOBHNA PHILIPS

Uganda - arrived 1972

My family lived in Kampala, the capital of Uganda. We were members of the Lohana community, though where we lived was very mixed. There were Patels and Hindu Punjabis, Muslims and some Arabic people as well. Our neighbours were Hindu Punjabis.

My family had 24 hours to get out of the country.

Then, in 1972, Idi Amin expelled all the Asians from Uganda. My family had 24 hours to get out of the country.

Shobhna now volunteers for a primary care team in Southampton and broadcasts on the community radio station Unity 101.

ROSE
DAWSON

Czechoslovakia - arrived 1939

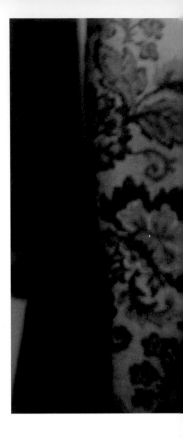

Rose was born in 1919 to a Jewish family in the Sudetenland area of Czechoslovakia and by 1939 she was working as a shorthand typist in Prague. After seeing Hitler's troops march into the city she contacted an organisation in the UK which helped refugees escape by placing them as servants in British households.

It was terrible, terrible saying goodbye.

Mum said 'You must go because there is no future for us here.' I had to wait a long time for my permit to come from England. Then I had to get my passport. I had to go to an office where the Gestapo were, and pay lots of money to get permission to leave. I left three days before the war; I didn't know it was so close.

I was told I was not allowed to take any money or jewellery, just clothes and nothing else. My family and friends saw me off at Prague station. It was terrible, terrible saying goodbye to them. In the train we got as far as Germany. The station was full of soldiers and they said 'Stop, no more trains tonight.' The Gestapo were everywhere so we had to get off the train and I saw somebody looking through someone else's case. So I wondered what to do, standing there with my case, and two soldiers approached me and I shrank a little, and they said 'Don't be afraid, we're not Gestapo, just ordinary soldiers,' and I said 'What am I going to do? I'm going to England.' They looked at each other and one went to speak to the station master and asked him if he would lock me in for the night in his waiting room, so that I could catch the next train. I had to go from there to Holland and from Holland to England by boat. I'll never forget them, they were so kind. I hope they survived the war.

When I arrived in Harwich there were lots of people with armbands waiting for the refugees, and they put us on a coach to London. We were taken to a guest house. I didn't have a phone number – just a name and address in Southampton. Then Mr Davis phoned up, he was a businessman and he had a big store in Southampton, and he said I should get a taxi to Waterloo. I waited there and he

turned up with his bowler hat – he knew what I looked like from my photograph. I was very near to tears but he had been in the First World War and he knew what it meant to be away from home. He was very kind to me.

I never found out what happened to my mother and one sister, but I guessed what happened.

While I was first in Southampton I wrote a letter home but it came back to me, stamped with 'Frontier Closed' so they never got the letter. I knew my family were in danger. I knew what was happening. Concentration camps – I'd heard of them. I never found out what happened to my mother and one sister, but I guessed what happened.

The family I stayed with were very kind to me. We moved out of Southampton to Rownhams because of the bombing. I had to go

to the police and ask permission if I wanted to go anywhere, and they would stamp my book – my Aliens Order. It didn't worry me. They had to be careful because so many different nationalities came to England. But when the Davis's moved again I couldn't go with them because of being an alien. Mr Davis pleaded with the police but they said they couldn't make any exceptions. They were very sorry.

At the suggestion of a friend, Rose moved to Basingstoke. She found a job working in a greenhouse, settled into lodgings and started seeing a young man called Bill.

Once we went to the pictures and the film was about a girl and a boy of different religions. When we got to my lodgings I started crying, and he said 'What's the matter?' and I said 'I have to tell you something, I'm of Jewish parentage.' He said 'Is that all? I thought you were going to say you had finished with me.' So I knew it was all right.

Then one day he came up to my room and said 'What would you say if one day I gave you a ring? Would you accept it?' And I said yes. And he had it ready in his pocket and said 'If you don't like it,

I said 'I have to tell you something.
I'm of Jewish parentage.' He said
'Is that all? I thought you were going
to say you had finished with me.'

I'll change it.' It's lovely, it has a blue stone, and I was so excited I went down and I said to my landlady 'Look what Bill gave me!' and she and her husband fetched a drop of wine. I nearly cry when I think about it. He was so decent even when we got engaged. There was never any hanky panky, we just kissed each other. We went to a Registry Office in Southampton. We were married in '43 and I became a British subject. After that I didn't need my Aliens card.

I came here when I was 18 and I'm 91 now.

Our first house together was this one. The three children all went to school in Southampton. I settled in very well, very quickly. I've forgotten a lot of my own language. I came here when I was 18 and I'm 91 now.

I've been here a lifetime.

BEYOND THE BOOK

Artist Lucy Gill and the
Talking Globe in progress

BEYOND THE BOOK

This is my home now is a project that combines oral history, a book, a touring exhibition and a website. The exhibition opened at The Art House in Southampton in June 2011. After showing at the Discovery Centre in Winchester in January 2012, it will be touring various Hampshire museums and venues.

Adam Hender and his team at Visible-Ideas Ltd have devised a remarkable audio-visual display for the exhibition – a 'talking globe'. This combines media, bespoke software and more traditional metalwork. The software allows visitors to listen to an interview extract from each of the refugees who have taken part in the project, while pinpointing their countries of origin. The metalwork is hand-made by artist Lucy Gill in mirrored stainless steel. Its shape takes reference from the Buckminster Fuller globe, a projection of the world's surface in the shape of an icosahedron, which can be unfolded or flattened to form a two-dimensional map while retaining the proportional integrity of a globe.

Through our website, www.myhomenow.org, also produced by Adam Hender, we hope to continue our project by inviting visitors to contribute their own stories of flight and sanctuary. We also provide a detailed record of the events and processes involved – a 'how-to' guide which we hope will benefit other groups and organisations.

Visit us online at www.myhomenow.org

ACKNOWLEDGEMENTS

The idea for collecting personal testimonies was initiated by Jenny Cuffe and arose from our shared interest and work as volunteers for Southampton & Winchester Visitors' Group, SWVG, which supports asylum seekers and refugees. We have also drawn on the expertise of CLEAR, City Life Education and Action for Refugees and been assisted by the welcoming team at Avenue St Andrews multicultural centre, also in Southampton.

Our project was inspired by a book of stories and photographs by Nikki van der Gaag and Rory Carnegie called *How the World Came to Oxford* and a Museum of London project, *Belonging: Voices of London's Refugees.*

We have shamelessly exploited the good will and talents of our creative team: Judith Heneghan, the writer who has deftly captured the speaking voices of our story-tellers, our photographer Fang Gleizes, Isabel Jameson who has designed this book and Ray Elmitt who has helped with the editing. SWVG members Shirley Firth, Xanthe Hackett and Auriol Mayo have conducted some of the interviews and we have benefited from the wisdom and knowledge of our steering group: Stephen Boyce, Padmini Broomfield, Anne Leeming and Paul Leppitt.

We are grateful to the Heritage Lottery Fund which has made this project possible. The entire collection of recorded interviews has been donated to Southampton City Council, one of our sponsors, for its archives. Southampton Solent University has kindly provided its photographic darkroom and printing facilities.

Above all, our thanks go to the 27 men and women who have so generously shared their stories with us.

Maïanna Moreau
Project Manager, *This is my home now*